365

Ways to Fight Daily Stress

ART COLOURING AND WISDOM TO LIFT YOUR SPIRIT

365
Ways to Fight Daily Stress

ART COLOURING AND WISDOM TO LIFT YOUR SPIRIT

WHITE STAR PUBLISHERS

INTRODUCTION

As we all know, daily life is marked by many small and great difficulties and obstacles which, even if they are often not insurmountable, accumulate day after day, creating the unpleasant feeling that today we call "stress." Frantic routines at frantic speed, tasks and deadlines, and everything has to work out, in some way... What is lacking, sometimes, is a moment to dedicate to ourselves, a little pause to free our mind, a pause in which we can express our creativity and again find a more harmonious rhythm of existence, more in accord with ourselves. In other words, the recovery of our interior well-being.

Fortunately, even a simple book can sometimes come to our aid and accompany us throughout the year. By using the principles of art therapy, a discipline that sees in the various forms of artistic creation a strong therapeutic anti-stress value, this volume will in fact offer you the opportunity to make use of your free time in an activity that is relaxing, highly fulfilling, and motivating. The collection of line drawings presented in these pages is already in itself a joy for the eyes, and constitutes, thanks to the variety of splendid details, a rich and gratifying anthology of themes and ornaments, symmetries, whirls, and intertwining designs... But it is by seeking to colour the drawings, according to your own personal taste and your imagination, that you will benefit from the positive charge deriving from artistic activity. You will have no limits, except those of your imagination, and once you have chosen whether to use crayons or felt-tips, the forms, the shapes, and the figures in the following pages will

magically come to life, by becoming the expression of your aesthetic taste and your colour preferences. Animals, flowers, and plants will come to life in a kaleidoscope of fantastic shades, like the abstract and geometrical figures that you will be able to decorate. You do not need particular technical abilities: well-being through art is within everyone's reach. You only require a good dose of patience, the right mixture of imagination and the desire to enjoy yourselves, by relaxing. The results will certainly astonish you and contribute at the same time to increasing your self-respect. But this book offers you more. Accompanying the plates to colour, there are illuminating and inspiring citations by famous people in the most diverse fields. From philosophers to men of faith, from politically engaged singers to actors, from artists to literary figures, even from scientists and statesmen, the great thoughts of great people will accompany your colouring activity, giving interesting points to reflect on, to reconsider preconceived ideas, to open up to new visions of reality. You will find a citation for every day of the year: it is a thought that will follow you in your daily life and that, at the end of the journey, will constitute an introspective path that you have made your own. In the same way, when you have coloured all the drawings, you will perceive them as a particularly intimate and personal expression; when you look at them again, we hope that you will be able to feel that they have helped you to recover that well-being, serenity, and inner peace that you were seeking.

1

"Look deep into nature, and then you will understand everything better."

– *Albert Einstein*

2

"It does not matter how slowly you go as long as you do not stop."

– *Confucius*

3

"Where there is love there is life."

– *Mahatma Gandhi*

4

"However difficult life may seem, there is always something you can do and succeed at."

– *Stephen Hawking*

5

"It is better to conquer yourself than to win a thousand battles. Then the victory is yours. It cannot be taken from you, not by angels or by demons, heaven or hell."

– *Buddha*

6

"There is nothing either good or bad but thinking makes it so."

– *William Shakespeare*

7

"Quality is not an act, it is a habit."

– *Aristotle*

8

"Start by doing what's necessary;
then do what's possible; and suddenly
you are doing the impossible."

– *Francis of Assisi*

9

"I can't change the direction of the wind,
but I can adjust my sails to always reach
my destination."

– *Jimmy Dean*

10

"Don't judge each day by the harvest you reap
but by the seeds that you plant."

— Robert Louis Stevenson

11

"Be kind whenever possible. It is always possible."

— Dalai Lama Tenzin Gyatso

12

"Whoever is happy will make others happy too."

— Anne Frank

13

"Do the difficult things while they are easy and do the great things while they are small. A journey of a thousand miles must begin with a single step."

— *Lao Tzu*

14

"Keep your eyes on the stars, and your feet on the ground."

— *Theodore Roosevelt*

15

"There is only one corner of the universe you can be certain of improving, and that's your own self."

— *Aldous Huxley*

16

"A good head and a good heart are always a formidable combination."

— *Nelson Mandela*

17

"We are shaped by our thoughts; we become what we think. When the mind is pure, joy follows like a shadow that never leaves."

— *Buddha*

18

"Who seeks shall find."

— *Sophocles*

19

> "Dream no small dreams for they have no power to move the hearts of men."
>
> — *Johann Wolfgang von Goethe*

20

> "All things must come to the soul from its roots, from where it is planted."
>
> — *Saint Teresa of Avila*

21

> "Don't be afraid to give up the good to go for the great."
>
> — *John D. Rockefeller*

22

"Change your life today.
Don't gamble on the future, act now, without delay."

– Simone de Beauvoir

23

"Love all, trust a few, do wrong to none."

– William Shakespeare

24

"I am not afraid… I was born to do this."

– Joan of Arc

25

"Never complain and never explain."

– Benjamin Disraeli

26

"It is not human nature we should accuse but the despicable conventions that pervert it."

– Denis Diderot

27

"Do not love leisure. Waste not a minute. Be bold. Realize the Truth, here and now!"

– Swami Sivananda

28

"Happy the man who has been able to learn the causes of things."

– Virgil

29

"I know of only one duty, and that is to love."

– Albert Camus

30

"Experience is simply the name we give our mistakes."

– Oscar Wilde

31

"Knowledge speaks, but wisdom listens."

– *Jimi Hendrix*

32

"It is not in the stars to hold our destiny
but in ourselves."

– *William Shakespeare*

33

"Our prime purpose in this life is to help
others. And if you can't help them,
at least don't hurt them."

– *Dalai Lama Tenzin Gyatso*

34

> "The only true wisdom is in knowing you know nothing."
>
> — *Socrates*

35

> "The two most powerful warriors are patience and time."
>
> — *Leo Tolstoy*

36

> "Colors, like features, follow the changes of the emotions."
>
> — *Pablo Picasso*

37

"The greater the obstacle, the more glory in overcoming it."

– *Molière*

38

"The will to win, the desire to succeed, the urge to reach your full potential… these are the keys that will unlock the door to personal excellence."

– *Confucius*

39

"Imperfection is beauty, madness is genius and it's better to be absolutely ridiculous than absolutely boring."

– *Marilyn Monroe*

40

"Nothing is enough for the man to whom enough is too little."

– Epicurus

41

"Do not overrate what you have received, nor envy others.
He who envies others does not obtain peace of mind."

– Buddha

42

"The true sign of intelligence is not knowledge but imagination."

– Albert Einstein

43

"Life is a journey.
When we stop, things don't go right."

– *Pope Francis*

44

"There are only two things. Truth and lies. Truth is indivisible, hence it cannot recognize itself; anyone who wants to recognize it has to be a lie."

– *Franz Kafka*

45

"Learning never exhausts the mind."

– *Leonardo da Vinci*

46

"The golden age is before us, not behind us."

— *William Shakespeare*

47

"Virtue has a veil, vice a mask."

— *Victor Hugo*

48

"Divide each difficulty into as many parts as is feasible and necessary to resolve it."

— *René Descartes*

49

"Confine yourself to the present."

– *Marcus Aurelius*

50

"There is no charm equal to tenderness of heart."

– *Jane Austen*

51

"Thousands of candles can be lighted from a single candle, and the life of the candle will not be shortened. Happiness never decreases by being shared."

– *Buddha*

52

"There is no duty we so much underrate as the duty of being happy. By being happy we sow anonymous benefits upon the world."

– Robert Louis Stevenson

53

"Do you wish to rise? Begin by descending. You plan a tower that will pierce the clouds? Lay first the foundation of humility."

– Saint Augustine

54

"Myths and creeds are heroic struggles
to comprehend the truth in the world."

— *Ansel Adams*

55

"The old believe everything,
the middle-aged suspect everything,
the young know everything."

— *Oscar Wilde*

56

"The world would be happier if men had the same capacity to be silent that they have to speak."

— *Baruch Spinoza*

57

"To know oneself, one should assert oneself."

— *Albert Camus*

58

"You can't wait for inspiration. You have to go after it with a club."

— *Jack London*

59

"To begin, begin."

– *William Wordsworth*

60

"If you can dream it, you can do it."

– *Walt Disney*

61

"Just as a candle cannot burn without fire,
men cannot live without a spiritual life."

– *Buddha*

62

"Love is composed of a single soul
inhabiting two bodies."

– Aristotle

63

"Pick the day. Enjoy it – to the hilt.
The day as it comes. People as they come..."

– Audrey Hepburn

64

"Efforts and courage are not enough
without purpose and direction."

– John F. Kennedy

65

"Try to be a rainbow in someone's cloud."

– Maya Angelou

66

"Always do your best. What you plant now,
you will harvest later."

– Og Mandino

67

"Cowards die many times before their deaths;
the valiant never taste of death but once."

– William Shakespeare

68

"A person who never made a mistake never tried anything new."

– *Albert Einstein*

69

"A friend is a gift you give yourself."

– *Robert Louis Stevenson*

70

"Happiness is not something ready made. It comes from your own actions."

– *Dalai Lama Tenzin Gyatso*

71

"In order to succeed, we must first believe that we can."

– *Nikos Kazantzakis*

72

"A jug fills drop by drop."

– *Buddha*

73

"Do you want to know who you are? Don't ask. Act! Action will delineate and define you."

– *Thomas Jefferson*

74

"Experience is not what happens to you; it's what you do with what happens to you."

– *Aldous Huxley*

75

"The key is to keep company only with people who uplift you, whose presence calls forth your best."

– *Epictetus*

76

"Ever tried. Ever failed. No matter. Try Again. Fail again. Fail better."

– *Samuel Beckett*

77

"There is no passion to be found playing small – in settling for a life that is less than the one you are capable of living."

– Nelson Mandela

78

"Life is really simple, but we insist on making it complicated."

– Confucius

79

"We are such stuff as dreams are made on; and our little life is rounded with a sleep."

– William Shakespeare

80

"Good, better, best. Never let it rest.
'Til your good is better and your
better is best."

— *St. Jerome*

81

"Knowing others is wisdom, knowing
yourself is Enlightenment."

— *Lao Tzu*

82

"What you get by achieving your goals
is not as important as what you become
by achieving your goals."

— *Henry David Thoreau*

83

"Do something wonderful, people may imitate it."

– Albert Schweitzer

84

"I attribute my success to this – I never gave or took any excuse."

– Florence Nightingale

85

"Knowing is not enough; we must apply. Willing is not enough; we must do."

– Johann Wolfgang von Goethe

86

"The final forming of a person's character lies in their own hands."

– Anne Frank

87

"Remember, if you ever need a helping hand, it's at the end of your arm, as you get older, remember you have another hand: The first is to help yourself, the second is to help others."

– Audrey Hepburn

88

"My best friend is the man who in wishing me well wishes it for my sake."

– Aristotle

89

"Intelligence is the ability to adapt
to change."

— *Stephen Hawking*

90

"Satisfaction lies in the effort, not in the
attainment, full effort is full victory."

— *Mahatma Gandhi*

91

"You are never too old to set another goal
or to dream a new dream."

— *C. S. Lewis*

92

"Consult not your fears but your hopes and your dreams.
Think not about your frustrations, but about your unfulfilled potential.
Concern yourself not with what you tried and failed in,
but with what it is still possible for you to do."

– *Pope John XXIII*

93

"I know where I'm going and I know the truth, and I don't have
to be what you want me to be. I'm free to be what I want."

– *Muhammad Ali*

94

"The secret of getting ahead is getting started."

– *Mark Twain*

95

"Motivation is the art of getting people
to do what you want them to do because
they want to do it."

– *Dwight D. Eisenhower*

96

"When truth has no burning, then it is philosophy, when it gets burning from the heart, it becomes poetry."

– Muhammad Iqbal

97

"The thought is a deed. Of all deeds she fertilizes the world most."

– Emile Zola

98

"Life is too short to be little. Man is never so manly as when he feels deeply, acts boldly, and expresses himself with frankness and with fervor."

– Benjamin Disraeli

99

"The most effective way to do it, is to do it."

– Amelia Earhart

100

"The empty vessel makes the loudest sound."

– *William Shakespeare*

101

"We cannot solve our problems with the same thinking we used when we created them."

– *Albert Einstein*

102

"The aim of art is to represent not the
outward appearance of things, but their
inward significance."

– *Aristotle*

103

"I never see what has been done;
I only see what remains to be done."

– *Buddha*

104

"The past cannot be changed. The future is yet in your power."

– *Mary Pickford*

105

"It is a golden maxim to cultivate the garden for the nose, and the eyes will take care of themselves."

– *Robert Louis Stevenson*

106

"One life is all we have and we live it as we believe in living it. But to sacrifice what you are and to live without belief, that is a fate more terrible than dying."

– *Joan of Arc*

107

"Most people spend more time and energy going around problems than in trying to solve them."

– *Henry Ford*

108

"It is very important to know who you are.
To make decisions. To show who you are."

– Malala Yousafzai

109

"Three things cannot be long hidden:
the sun, the moon, and the truth."

– Buddha

110

"Do not wait to strike till the iron is hot;
but make it hot by striking."

– William Butler Yeats

111

"You have to make it happen."

—*Denis Diderot*

112

"Always do good to others. Be selfless. Mentally remove everything and be free. This is divine life. This is the direct way to Moksha or salvation."

— *Swami Sivananda*

113

"Ignorance is the curse of God; knowledge is the wing wherewith we fly to heaven."

— *William Shakespeare*

114

"Anticipate the difficult by managing the easy."

– Lao Tzu

115

"Love conquers all."

– Virgil

116

"In the practice of tolerance, one's enemy is the best teacher."

– Dalai Lama Tenzin Gyatso

117

"Real generosity toward the future lies
in giving all to the present."

– *Albert Camus*

118

"Every day we should hear at least one little
song, read one good poem, see one exquisite
picture, and, if possible, speak
a few sensible words."

– *Johann Wolfgang von Goethe*

119

"Perseverance is not a long race; it is many
short races one after the other."

– *Walter Elliot*

120

"Choose a job you love, and you will never have to work a day in your life."

– *Confucius*

121

"The mind is everything. What you think you become."

– *Buddha*

122

"Man approaches the unattainable truth through a succession of errors."

– *Aldous Huxley*

123

"From a small seed a mighty trunk may grow."

— *Aeschylus*

124

"The evil that is in the world almost always comes of ignorance, and good intentions may do as much harm as malevolence if they lack understanding."

— *Albert Camus*

125

"Peace is not an absence of war, it is a virtue, a state of mind, a disposition for benevolence, confidence, justice."

— *Baruch Spinoza*

126

"Keep love in your heart. A life without it is like a sunless garden when the flowers are dead."

– Oscar Wilde

127

"Either move or be moved."

– Ezra Pound

128

"Try not to become a man of success, but rather try to become a man of value."

– Albert Einstein

129

"With realization of one's own potential and self-confidence in one's ability, one can build a better world."

— *Dalai Lama Tenzin Gyatso*

130

"There is only one way to happiness and that is to cease worrying about things which are beyond the power of our will."

— *Epictetus*

131

"No man has the right to dictate what other men should perceive, create or produce, but all should be encouraged to reveal themselves, their perceptions and emotions, and to build confidence in the creative spirit."

— *Ansel Adams*

132

"The purpose of human life is to serve, and to show compassion and the will to help others."

– *Albert Schweitzer*

133

"We are all instruments endowed with feeling and memory. Our senses are so many strings that are struck by surrounding objects and that also frequently strike themselves."

– *Denis Diderot*

134

"We may encounter many defeats but we must not be defeated."

– *Maya Angelou*

135

"Some are born great, some achieve greatness,
and some have greatness thrust upon them."

— *William Shakespeare*

136

"Silence is a true friend who never betrays."

— *Confucius*

136

"If you talk to a man in a language he understands, that goes to his head.
If you talk to him in his language, that goes to his heart."

– *Nelson Mandela*

137

"The world is a book, and those who do not travel read only a page."

– *Saint Augustine*

139

"Life is not a matter of holding good cards,
but of playing a poor hand well."

— *Robert Louis Stevenson*

140

"When you arise in the morning, think of
what a precious privilege it is to be alive –
to breathe, to think, to enjoy, to love."

— *Marcus Aurelius*

141

"I wish that every human life might be pure transparent freedom."

— *Simone de Beauvoir*

142

"Rather fail with honor than succeed by fraud."

— *Sophocles*

143

"You can't build a reputation on what
you are going to do."

– Henry Ford

144

"If you shut up truth, and bury
it underground, it will but grow."

– Emile Zola

145

"Memory is the mother of all wisdom."

– Aeschylus

146

"A dreamer is one who can only find his way by moonlight, and his punishment is that he sees the dawn before the rest of the world."

– *Oscar Wilde*

147

"The very substance of the ambitious is merely the shadow of a dream."

– *William Shakespeare*

148

"No one is so brave that he is not disturbed by something unexpected."

– *Julius Caesar*

149

"The noblest pleasure is the joy
of understanding."

– *Leonardo da Vinci*

150

"There is no blue without yellow
and without orange."

– *Vincent van Gogh*

151

"Grace is not part of consciousness;
it is the amount of light in our souls,
not knowledge nor reason."

– *Pope Francis*

152

"We know what we are, but know not what we may be."

– *William Shakespeare*

153

"The past, like the future, is indefinite and exists only as a spectrum of possibilities."

– *Stephen Hawking*

154

"The innocent and the beautiful have no enemy but time."

– *William Butler Yeats*

155

"Endure the present, and watch for better things."

– *Virgil*

156

"You will never be happy if you continue
to search for what happiness consists of.
You will never live if you are looking for
the meaning of life."

– *Albert Camus*

157

"There is something good in all seeming
failures. You are not to see that now.
Time will reveal it. Be patient."

– *Swami Sivananda*

158

"I hear and I forget. I see and I remember.
I do and I understand."

– *Confucius*

159

"One must ask children and birds
how cherries and strawberries taste."

– *Johann Wolfgang von Goethe*

160

"Start with what is right rather than
what is acceptable."

– *Franz Kafka*

161

"We are all travelers in the wilderness of this world, and the best we can find in our travels is an honest friend."

– *Robert Louis Stevenson*

162

"The more I see the less I know for sure."

– *John Lennon*

163

"The very essence of instinct is that it's followed independently of reason."

– *Charles Darwin*

164

"I find hope in the darkest of days, and focus in the brightest. I do not judge the universe."

– *Dalai Lama Tenzin Gyatso*

165

"It is true that we are made of dust.
And the world is also made of dust.
But the dust has motes rising."

– *Muhammad Iqbal*

166

"If you want to succeed you should strike out on new paths, rather than travel the worn paths of accepted success."

– *John D. Rockefeller*

167

"Except our own thoughts, there is nothing absolutely in our power."

– René Descartes

168

"The energy of the mind is the essence of life."

– Aristotle

169

"When I let go of what I am,
I become what I might be."

– Lao Tzu

170

"Success is not the key to happiness.
Happiness is the key to success.
If you love what you are doing,
you will be successful."

– *Albert Schweitzer*

171

"Simplicity is the ultimate sophistication."

– *Leonardo da Vinci*

172

"How far that little candle throws its beams!
So shines a good deed in a naughty world."

– *William Shakespeare*

173

"Do not spoil what you have by desiring what you have not;
remember that what you now have was once among
the things you only hoped for."

– *Epicurus*

174

"Anyone who keeps the ability to see beauty never grows old."

– *Franz Kafka*

175

"The greater danger for most of us lies not in setting our aim too high and falling short; but in setting our aim too low, and achieving our mark."

– *Michelangelo*

176

"Speak the truth, do not yield to anger; give, if thou art asked for little; by these three steps thou wilt go near the gods."

– *Confucius*

177

"Study nature, love nature, stay close
to nature. It will never fail you."

– *Frank Lloyd Wright*

178

"There are only two mistakes one can make
along the road to truth; not going all the way,
and not starting."

– *Buddha*

179

"Accustom yourself continually to make many acts of love, for they enkindle and melt the soul."

– Saint Teresa of Avila

180

"The roots of education are bitter, but the fruit is sweet."

– Aristotle

181

"The only source of knowledge is experience."

– Albert Einstein

182

"You can have no dominion greater or less
than that over yourself."

– *Leonardo da Vinci*

183

"Peace comes from within.
Do not seek it without."

– *Buddha*

184

"Strength does not come from physical capacity.
It comes from an indomitable will."

– *Mahatma Gandhi*

185

"You will never do anything in this world without courage. It is the greatest quality of the mind next to honor."

– *Aristotle*

186

"One isn't necessarily born with courage, but one is born with potential. Without courage, we cannot practice any other virtue with consistency. We can't be kind, true, merciful, generous, or honest."

– *Maya Angelou*

187

"Nothing is worth more than this day."

– *Johann Wolfgang von Goethe*

188

"It takes a long time to become young."

– *Pablo Picasso*

189

"What would life be if we had no courage
to attempt anything?"

– *Vincent van Gogh*

190

"First say to yourself what you would be;
and then do what you have to do."

– *Epictetus*

191

"No legacy is so rich as honesty."

– *William Shakespeare*

192

"You can give without loving, but you can never love without giving."

– *Robert Louis Stevenson*

193

"After climbing a great hill, one only finds that there are many more hills to climb."

– *Nelson Mandela*

194

"Hell isn't merely paved with good intentions; it's walled and roofed with them. Yes, and furnished too."

– *Aldous Huxley*

195

"Everything we hear is an opinion, not a fact. Everything we see is a perspective, not the truth."

– *Marcus Aurelius*

196

"Persevere and preserve yourselves for better circumstances."

– *Virgil*

197

"Most people say that it is the intellect
which makes a great scientist.
They are wrong: it is character."

– *Albert Einstein*

198

"The greatest wealth is to live content
with little."

– *Plato*

199

"Everyone thinks of changing the world,
but no one thinks of changing himself."

— *Leo Tolstoy*

200

"Education is not the filling of a pail,
but the lighting of a fire."

— *William Butler Yeats*

201

"In order to carry a positive action we must develop here a positive vision."

– *Dalai Lama Tenzin Gyatso*

202

"If your only goal is to become rich, you will never achieve it."

– *John D. Rockefeller*

203

"Wisdom outweighs any wealth."

– *Sophocles*

204

"My best friend is the one who brings out the best in me."

– *Henry Ford*

205

"If you ask me what I came into this life to do, I will tell you: I came to live out loud."

– *Emile Zola*

206

"Excessive fear is always powerless."

– *Aeschylus*

207

"Our ambition should be to rule ourselves,
the true kingdom for each one of us; and
true progress is to know more, and be
more, and to do more."

– Oscar Wilde

208

"Art is never finished, only abandoned."

– Leonardo da Vinci

209

"It is health that is the real wealth
and not pieces of gold and silver."

– Mahatma Gandhi

210

"All children are artists. The problem is how to remain an artist once he grows up."

– *Pablo Picasso*

211

"To know what you know and what you do not know, that is true knowledge."

– *Confucius*

212

"How poor are they that have not patience!
What wound did ever heal but by degrees?"

– *William Shakespeare*

213

"People won't have time for you if you are
always angry or complaining."

– *Stephen Hawking*

214

"It is in pardoning that we are pardoned."

– *Francis of Assisi*

215

"The best thing to hold onto in life
is each other."

– *Audrey Hepburn*

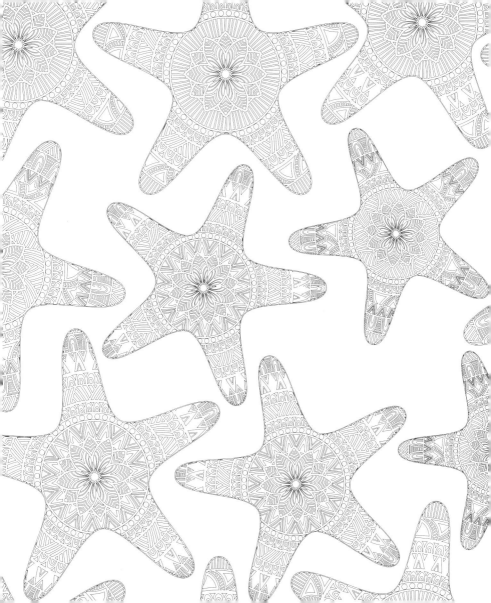

216

"The key to growth is the introduction of higher dimensions of consciousness into our awareness."

– *Lao Tzu*

217

"Whoever neglects the arts when he is young has lost the past and is dead to the future."

– *Sophocles*

218

"Talent perceives differences; genius, unity."

– *William Butler Yeats*

219

"However many holy words you read, however many you speak, what good will they do you if you do not act on upon them?"

– *Buddha*

220

"The habit of being happy enables one to be freed, or largely freed, from the domination of outward conditions."

– *Robert Louis Stevenson*

221

"Sometimes our light goes out but is blown into flame by another human being. Each of us owes deepest thanks to those who have rekindled this light."

– *Albert Schweitzer*

222

"Obstacles are those frightful things you see when you take your eyes off your goal."

– *Henry Ford*

223

"I am little concerned with beauty or perfection.
I don't care for the great centuries.
All I care about is life, struggle, intensity."

– *Emile Zola*

224

"I have the simplest tastes. I am always satisfied with the best."

– *Oscar Wilde*

225

"Do not weep; do not wax indignant. Understand."

– *Baruch Spinoza*

226

"A well-spent day brings happy sleep."

– *Leonardo da Vinci*

227

"It is no use walking anywhere to preach unless our walking is our preaching."

– *Francis of Assisi*

228

"If evil be spoken of you and it be true,
correct yourself; if it be a lie, laugh at it."

– *Epictetus*

229

"Love and compassion are necessities,
not luxuries. Without them humanity
cannot survive."

– *Dalai Lama Tenzin Gyatso*

230

"This above all: to thine own self be true."

– *William Shakespeare*

231

"Life is the flower for which love is the honey."

– Victor Hugo

232

"He who learns but does not think is lost!
He who thinks but does not learn
is in great danger."

– Confucius

233

"There are times when fear is good. It must
keep its watchful place at the heart's controls."

– Aeschylus

234

"One secret of success in life is for a man to be ready for his opportunity when it comes."

— *Benjamin Disraeli*

235

"Much wisdom often goes with fewest words."

— *Sophocles*

236

"No one saves us but ourselves.
No one can and no one may.
We ourselves must walk the path."

— *Buddha*

237

"False face must hide what the false
heart doth know."

– *William Shakespeare*

238

"First learn the meaning of what you say,
and then speak."

– *Epictetus*

239

"The man with insight enough to admit his
limitations comes nearest to perfection."

– *Johann Wolfgang von Goethe*

240

"Whoever is careless with the truth
in small matters cannot be trusted
with important matters."

– *Albert Einstein*

241

"Virtuous people often revenge themselves
for the constraints to which they submit
by the boredom which they inspire."

– *Confucius*

242

"Trust not too much to appearances."

– *Virgil*

243

"Love is of all passions the strongest,
for it attacks simultaneously the head,
the heart and the senses."

– Lao Tzu

244

"Our bodies are our gardens–
our wills are our gardeners."

– William Shakespeare

245

"Every heart that has beat strongly and
cheerfully has left a hopeful impulse behind
it in the world, and bettered the tradition
of mankind."

– Robert Louis Stevenson

246

"When anger rises, think of the consequences."

— *Confucius*

247

"No one has ever become poor by giving."

— *Anne Frank*

248

"We must use time wisely and forever realize that the time is always ripe to do right."

— *Nelson Mandela*

249

"You will not be punished for your anger,
you will be punished by your anger."

– Buddha

250

"More compassionate mind, more sense
of concern for other's well-being,
is source of happiness."

– Dalai Lama Tenzin Gyatso

251

"Men of ill judgment ignore the good that
lies within their hands, till they have lost it."

– Sophocles

252

"Society exists only as a mental concept;
in the real world there are only individuals."

– *Oscar Wilde*

253

"Measure what is measurable, and make
measurable what is not so."

– *Galileo Galilei*

254

"Youth has no age."

– *Pablo Picasso*

255

"The difference between stupidity and
genius is that genius has its limits."

– *Albert Einstein*

256

"Brevity is the soul of wit."

– *William Shakespeare*

257

"First they ignore you, then they laugh at you,
then they fight you, then you win."

– *Mahatma Gandhi*

258

"If you want to be happy, be."

– *Leo Tolstoy*

259

"While you are proclaiming peace with your lips, be careful to have it even more fully in your heart."

– *Francis of Assisi*

260

"Accept the things to which fate binds you, and love the people with whom fate brings you together, but do so with all your heart."

– *Marcus Aurelius*

261

"Be gentle to all and stern with yourself."

— *Saint Teresa of Avila*

262

"If you look into your own heart, and you find nothing wrong there, what is there to worry about? What is there to fear?"

— *Confucius*

263

"The worst form of inequality is to try to make unequal things equal."

— *Aristotle*

264

"No man is free who is not master of himself."

– *Epictetus*

265

"That men do not learn very much from the lessons of history is the most important of all the lessons of history."

– *Aldous Huxley*

266

"Better a witty fool than a foolish wit."

– *William Shakespeare*

267

"Happiness is neither virtue nor pleasure
nor this thing nor that but simply growth,
We are happy when we are growing."

– William Butler Yeats

268

"The best way to resolve any problem
in the human world is for all sides to sit
down and talk."

– Dalai Lama Tenzin Gyatso

269

"None are more hopelessly enslaved than
those who falsely believe they are free."

– Johann Wolfgang von Goethe

270

"Tolerance implies no lack of commitment to one's own beliefs. Rather it condemns the oppression or persecution of others."

– *John F. Kennedy*

271

"Let us remember: One book, one pen, one child, and one teacher can change the world."

– *Malala Yousafzai*

272

"Time brings all things to pass."

– *Aeschylus*

273

"Work out your own salvation.
Do not depend on others."

– Buddha

274

"If you want to improve, be content to be
thought foolish and stupid."

– Epictetus

275

"Nothing will work unless you do."

– Maya Angelou

276

"Love begets love, love knows no rules,
this is same for all."

– *Virgil*

277

"Crave for a thing, you will get it.
Renounce the craving, the object
will follow you by itself."

– *Swami Sivananda*

278

"What's done can't be undone."

— *William Shakespeare*

279

"Let us make our future now,
and let us make our dreams
tomorrow's reality."

— *Malala Yousafzai*

280

"Never give a sword to a man who can't dance."

– Confucius

281

"One who knows how to show and to accept kindness will be a friend better than any possession."

– Sophocles

282

"Failure is simply the opportunity to begin again, this time more intelligently."

– Henry Ford

283

"Where there is charity and wisdom,
there is neither fear nor ignorance."

– *Francis of Assisi*

284

"In nature we never see anything isolated,
but everything in connection with
something else which is before it,
beside it, under it and over it."

– *Johann Wolfgang von Goethe*

285

"Never apologize for showing feeling.
When you do so, you apologize for the truth."

– *Benjamin Disraeli*

286

"But time growing old teaches all things."

– Aeschylus

287

"Hatred does not cease by hatred, but only by love; this is the eternal rule."

– Buddha

288

"Example is leadership."

– Albert Schweitzer

289

"All our knowledge has its origins in our perceptions."

– *Leonardo da Vinci*

290

"We can live without religion and meditation, but we cannot survive without human affection."

– *Dalai Lama Tenzin Gyatso*

291

"I believe things cannot make themselves impossible."

– *Stephen Hawking*

292

"It is impossible to live a pleasant life
without living wisely and well and justly.
And it is impossible to live wisely and well
and justly without living a pleasant life."

— *Epicurus*

293

"A fool thinks himself to be wise,
but a wise man knows himself to be a fool."

— *William Shakespeare*

294

"Waste no more time arguing about what
a good man should be. Be one."

— *Marcus Aurelius*

295

"Wisdom, compassion, and courage
are the three universally recognized
moral qualities of men."

– Confucius

296

"The fishermen know that the sea is
dangerous and the storm terrible, but they
have never found these dangers sufficient
reason for remaining ashore."

– Vincent van Gogh

297

"There are two things a person should
never be angry at: what they can help,
and what they cannot."

– Plato

298

"There is nothing like returning to a place that remains unchanged to find the ways in which you yourself have altered."

— *Nelson Mandela*

299

"Only two things are infinite, the universe and human stupidity, and I'm not sure about the former."

— *Albert Einstein*

300

"To be what we are, and to become what we are capable of becoming, is the only end of life."

— *Robert Louis Stevenson*

301

"A man may die, nations may rise and fall, but an idea lives on."

– *John F. Kennedy*

302

"No one is to be called an enemy, all are your benefactors, and no one does you harm. You have no enemy except yourselves."

– *Francis of Assisi*

303

"It is a man's own mind, not his enemy
or foe, that lures him to evil ways."

– *Buddha*

304

"It is the nature of the self to manifest itself.
In every atom slumbers the might of the self."

– *Muhammad Iqbal*

305

"Live as if you were to die tomorrow. Learn as if you were to live forever."

— *Mahatma Gandhi*

306

"Happiness depends upon ourselves."

— *Aristotle*

307

"As we express our gratitude, we must never forget that the highest appreciation is not to utter words, but to live by them."

— *John F. Kennedy*

308

"Truthful words are not beautiful; beautiful words are not truthful. Good words are not persuasive; persuasive words are not good."

– Lao Tzu

309

"The purpose of art is washing the dust of daily life off our souls."

– Pablo Picasso

310

"Listen to many, speak to a few."

– William Shakespeare

311

"If you have done terrible things, you must endure terrible things; for thus the sacred light of injustice shines bright."

– *Sophocles*

312

"Look at situations from all angles, and you will become more open."

– *Dalai Lama Tenzin Gyatso*

313

"Keep silence for the most part, and speak only when you must, and then briefly."

– *Epictetus*

314

"Our greatest glory is not in never falling,
but in rising every time we fall."

– *Confucius*

315

"Success is like reaching an important
birthday and finding you're exactly
the same."

– *Audrey Hepburn*

316

"I am prepared for the worst,
but hope for the best."

– *Benjamin Disraeli*

317

"The body is a house of many windows: there we all sit, showing ourselves and crying on the passers-by to come and love us."

– *Robert Louis Stevenson*

318

"It is best for the wise man not to seem wise."

– *Aeschylus*

319

"The only difference between the saint
and the sinner is that every saint has a past,
and every sinner has a future."

– *Oscar Wilde*

320

"Great things are done by a series of small
things brought together."

– *Vincent van Gogh*

321

"The only real failure in life is not to be true to the best one knows."

– *Buddha*

322

"You have to learn the rules of the game. And then you have to play better than anyone else."

– *Albert Einstein*

323

"Love is the greatest refreshment in life."

– *Pablo Picasso*

324

"One of the first conditions of happiness is that the link between Man and Nature shall not be broken."

– *Leo Tolstoy*

325

"Beginning today, treat everyone you meet as if they were going to be dead by midnight. Extend to them all the care, kindness and understanding you can muster, and do it with no thought of any reward. Your life will never be the same again."

– *Og Mandino*

326

"Life belongs to the living, and he who lives must be prepared for changes."

– *Johann Wolfgang von Goethe*

327

"Only the wisest and stupidest of men never change."

– *Confucius*

328

"We all have to live together, so we might as well live together happily."

– *Dalai Lama Tenzin Gyatso*

329

"When one's expectations are reduced to zero, one really appreciates everything one does have."

– *Stephen Hawking*

330

"The great enemy of the truth is very often not the lie, deliberate, contrived and dishonest, but the myth, persistent, persuasive and unrealistic."

– *John F. Kennedy*

331

"Love is the beauty of the soul."

– *Saint Augustine*

332

"Courageous people do not fear forgiving, for the sake of peace."

– *Nelson Mandela*

333

"Fortune favors the bold."

— *Virgil*

334

"The man that hath no music in himself,
nor is not moved with concord of sweet sounds,
is fit for treasons, stratagems and spoils."

— *William Shakespeare*

335

"Keep your fears to yourself,
but share your courage with others."

— *Robert Louis Stevenson*

336

"The weak can never forgive.
Forgiveness is the attribute of the strong."

— *Mahatma Gandhi*

337

"We should feel sorrow, but not sink under its oppression."

— *Confucius*

338

"Our greatest weakness lies in giving up.
The most certain way to succeed is always to try just one more time."

— *Thomas A. Edison*

339

"Better than a thousand hollow words,
is one word that brings peace."

— *Buddha*

340

"Come what may, all bad fortune is to be
conquered by endurance."

— *Virgil*

341

"Every good act is charity. A man's true
wealth hereafter is the good that he does
in this world to his fellows."

— *Molière*

342

"For it is in giving that we receive."

– Francis of Assisi

343

"Reality leaves a lot to the imagination."

– John Lennon

344

"Learn from yesterday, live for today, hope for tomorrow. The important thing is not to stop questioning."

– Albert Einstein

345

"Truth, like gold, is to be obtained not by
its growth, but by washing away from it all
that is not gold."

— *Leo Tolstoy*

346

"The world turns aside to let any man pass
who knows where he is going."

— *Epictetus*

347

"The secret of genius is to carry the spirit
of the child into old age, which mean never
losing your enthusiasm."

— *Aldous Huxley*

348

"Every act of rebellion expresses a nostalgia for innocence and an appeal to the essence of being."

– *Albert Camus*

349

"There are three methods to gaining wisdom. The first is reflection, which is the highest. The second is limitation, which is the easiest. The third is experience, which is the bitterest."

– *Confucius*

350

"You have power over your mind – not outside events. Realize this, and you will find strength."

– *Marcus Aurelius*

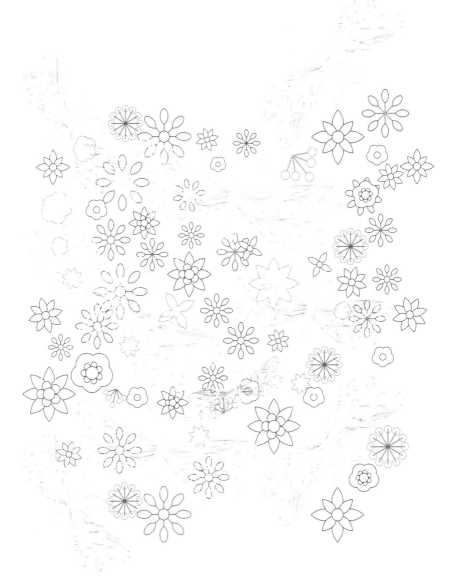

351

"No great artist ever sees things as they really are. If he did, he would cease to be an artist."

– *Oscar Wilde*

352

"I would prefer even to fail with honor than win by cheating."

– *Sophocles*

353

"I always tried to turn every disaster into an opportunity."

– *John D. Rockefeller*

354

"We live in fear and therefore we don't live."

– *Buddha*

355

"Rise above sectional interests and private
ambitions… Pass from matter to spirit.
Matter is diversity; spirit is light,
life and unity."

– *Muhammad Iqbal*

356

"We are all so much together, but we are all
dying of loneliness."

– *Albert Schweitzer*

357

"There is nothing insignificant in the world.
It all depends on the point of view."

– Johann Wolfgang von Goethe

358

"In all things of nature there is something of the marvelous."

– Aristotle

359

"He who knows that enough is enough will always have enough."

– Lao Tzu

360

"If you don't like something, change it.
If you can't change it, change your attitude.
Don't complain."

– *Maya Angelou*

361

"You gotta try your luck at least once a day,
because you could be going around lucky
all day and not even know it."

– *Jimmy Dean*

362

"I say there is no darkness but ignorance."

– *William Shakespeare*

363

"How wonderful it is that nobody need wait a single moment before starting to improve the world."

– *Anne Frank*

364

"Scientists have become the bearers of the torch of discovery in our quest for knowledge."

– *Stephen Hawking*

365

"When you practice gratefulness, there is a sense of respect toward others."

– *Dalai Lama Tenzin Gyatso*

List of contributors

A

Adams, Ansel, 1902-1984, American photographer (54, 131)

Aeschylus, 525-456 B.C., Greek playwright (123, 145, 206, 233, 272, 286, 318)

Angelou, Maya, 1928-2014, American poet, painter and dancer (65, 134, 186, 275, 360)

Aristotle, 384/383-322 B.C., Greek philosopher (62, 88, 102, 168, 180, 185, 263, 306, 358)

Augustine of Hippo, Saint, 354-430, Roman philosopher, bishop and theologian (53, 137, 331)

Aurelius, Marcus Antoninus Augustus, 121-180, Roman emperor, philosopher and writer (49, 140, 195, 260, 294, 350)

Austen, Jane, 1775-1817, English writer (50)

B

Beckett, Samuel, 1906-1989, Irish writer, playwright, poet and theater director (76)

Buddha, Siddhārtha Gautama, VI century B.C., founder of Buddhism (5, 17, 41, 51, 61, 72, 103, 109, 121, 178, 183, 219, 236, 249, 273, 287, 303, 321, 339, 354)

Buonarroti, Michelangelo, 1475-1564, Italian sculptor, painter, architect and poet (175)

C

Caesar, Gaius Julius, 100-44 B.C., Roman statesman, orator and author (148)

Camus, Albert, 1913-1960, French writer, philosopher, essayist, playwright (29, 57, 117, 124, 156, 348)

Confucius, 551-479 B.C., Chinese philosopher (2, 38, 78, 120, 136, 158, 176, 211, 232, 241, 246, 262, 280, 295, 314, 327, 337, 349)

D

Dalai Lama Tenzin Gyatso, 1935-, Tibetan Buddhist monk (11, 33, 70, 116, 129, 164, 201, 229, 250, 268, 290, 312, 328, 365)

Darwin, Charles, 1809-1882, English biologist and naturalist (163)

Da Vinci, Leonardo, 1452-1519, Italian painter, engineer and scientist (45, 149, 171, 182, 208, 226, 289)

Dean, Jimmy, 1928-2010, American actor (9, 361)

De Beauvoir, Simone, 1908-1986, French writer, essayist, philosopher and feminist (22, 141)

Descartes, René, 1596-1650, French philosopher and mathematician (48, 167)

Diderot, Denis, 1713-1784, French philosopher and writer (26, 111, 133)

Disney, Walter ("Walt") Elias, 1901-1966, American

businessman, movie producer and director (60)

Disraeli, Benjamin, 1804-1881, English politician and writer (25, 98, 234, 285, 316)

E

Earhart, Amelia, 1897-1937, American aviator (99)

Edison, Thomas Alva, 1847-1931, American inventor and businessman (338)

Einstein, Albert, 1879-1955, German physician and philosopher (1, 42, 68, 101, 128, 181, 197, 240, 255, 299, 322, 344)

Eisenhower, Dwight David, 1890-1969, General and thirty-fourth president of United States of America (95)

Elliot, Walter, 1888-1958, Scottish politician (119)

Epictetus, around 50 - 130, Greek philosopher (75, 130, 190, 228, 238, 264, 274, 313, 346)

Epicurus, 342-270 B.C., Greek philosopher (40, 173, 292)

F

Ford, Henry, 1863-1947, American businessman (107, 143, 204, 222, 282)

Francis, Pope (Jorge Mario Bergoglio), 1936-, Pope of the Roman Catholic Church (43, 151)

Francis of Assisi, Saint, 1182-1226, Italian saint and poet (8, 214, 227, 259, 283, 302, 342)

Frank, Anne, 1929-1945, German Jewish victim of Shoah (12, 86, 247, 363)

G

Galilei, Galileo, 1564-1642, Italian physician, philosopher, astronomer and mathematician (253)

Gandhi, Mahatma (Mohandas Karamchand), 1869-1948, Indian politician and philosopher (3, 90, 184, 209, 257, 305, 336)

Goethe, Johann Wolfgang von 1749-1832, German poet and writer (19, 85, 118, 159, 187, 239, 269, 284, 326, 357)

Gogh, Vincent van, 1853-1890, Dutch painter (150, 189, 296, 320)

H

Hawking, Stephen William, 1942-, English physician, mathematician, cosmologist, astrophysicist and writer (4, 89, 153, 213, 291, 329, 364)

Hendrix, Jimi, 1942-1970, American guitarist and singer-songwriter (31)

Hepburn, Audrey (Ruston, Audrey Kathleen), 1929-1993, English actress (63, 87, 215, 315)

Hugo, Victor, 1802-1885, French poet, playwright, painter and writer (47, 231)

Huxley, Aldous, 1894-1963, English writer (15, 74, 122, 194, 265, 347)

I

Iqbal, Muhammad, 1877-1938, Pakistani scholar, poet, philosopher and columnist (96, 165, 304, 355)

J

Jefferson, Thomas, 1743-1826, American politician, scientist and architect (73)

Joan of Arc, Saint, 1412-1431, French national heroine (24, 106)

John XXIII, Pope (Angelo Giuseppe Roncalli), 1881-1963, Pope of the Roman Catholic Church (92)

K

Kafka, Franz, 1883-1924, Czechoslovakian-Bohemian writer (44, 160, 174)

Kazantzakis, Nikos, 1883-1957, Greek writer, poet, journalist and philosopher (71)

Kennedy, John Fitzgerald, 1917-1963, thirty-fifth president of United States of America (64, 270, 301, 307, 330)

L

Lao, Tzu, VI century B.C., Chinese philosopher (13, 81, 114, 169, 216, 243, 308, 359)

Lennon, John, 1940-1980, English singer-songwriter, poet and activist (162, 343)

Lewis, Clive Staples, 1898-1963, English writer and philologist (91)

London, Jack (London, John Griffith Chaney), American writer (58)

M

Mandela, Nelson, 1918-2013, president of South Africa and Nobel Peace Prize Laureate (16, 77, 136, 193, 248, 298, 332)

Mandino, Og, 1923-1996, American author (66, 325)

Molière (Poquelin, Jean-Baptiste), 1622-1673, French comedy writer and actor (37, 341)

Monroe, Marilyn (Mortenson, Norma Jeane), 1926-1962, American actress (39)

Muhammad Ali (Cassius Marcellus Clay), 1942-, American boxer (93)

N

Nightingale, Florence, 1820-1910, English modern nursing pioneer and writer (84)

P

Picasso, Pablo, 1881-1973, Spanish painter, sculptor and lithographer (36, 188, 210, 254, 309, 323)

Pickford, Mary, 1892-1979, Canadian actress (104)

Plato, 428/427-348/347 B.C., Greek philosopher (198, 297)

Pound, Ezra Weston Loomis, 1885-1972, American poet, essayist, and translator (127)

R

Rockefeller, John D., 1839-1937, American businessman and philanthropist (21, 166, 202, 353)

Roosevelt, Theodore, 1858-

1919, twenty-sixth president of the United States of America (14)

S

Saraswati, Sivananda Swami, 1887-1963, Indian philosopher and writer (27, 112, 157, 227)

Schweitzer, Albert, 1875-1965, French-German Lutheran doctor, musician, philosopher, missionary and theologian (83, 132, 170, 221, 288, 356)

Shakespeare, William, 1564-1616, English poet and writer (6, 23, 32, 46, 67, 79, 100, 113, 135, 147, 152, 172, 191, 212, 230, 237, 244, 256, 266, 278, 293, 310, 334, 362)

Socrates, 470/469-399 B.C., Greek philosopher (34)

Sophocles, 496-406 B.C., Greek playwright (18, 142, 203, 217, 235, 251, 281, 311, 352)

Sophronius Eusebius Jerome, Saint, 347-419/420, Roman writer and theologian (80)

Spinoza, Baruch, 1632-1677, Dutch philosopher (56, 125, 225)

Stevenson, Robert Louis Balfour, 1850-1894, Scottish writer (10, 52, 69, 105, 139, 161, 192, 220, 245, 300, 317, 335)

T

Teresa of Avila, Saint, 1515-1582, Spanish religious woman and mystic (20, 179, 261)

Thoreau, Henry David, 1817-1862, American philosopher, writer and poet (82)

Tolstoy, Leo Nikolàevič, 1828-1910, Russian writer and philosopher (35, 199, 258, 324, 345)

Twain, Mark (Clemens, Samuel Langhorne), 1835-1910, American writer, humorist and teacher (94)

V

Virgil, Maro Publius, 70-19 B.C., Roman poet (28, 115, 155, 196, 242, 276, 333, 340)

W

Wilde, Oscar, 1854-1900, Irish writer, poet, journalist and essayist (30, 55, 126, 146, 207, 224, 252, 319, 351)

Wordsworth, William, 1770-1850, English poet (59)

Wright, Frank Lloyd, 1867-1959, American architect (177)

Y

Yeats, William Butler, 1865-1939, Irish poet and writer (110, 154, 200, 218, 267)

Yousafzai, Malala, 1997-, Pakistani Nobel Peace Prize Laureate, student and activist (108, 271, 279)

Z

Zola, Émile Édouard Charles Antoine, 1840-1902, French writer, journalist, essayist and literary critic (97, 144, 205, 223)

Photo Credits

All illustrations are reworkings of images drawn
from 123RF, iStockphoto and Shutterstock

Graphic Design

Paola Piacco

WS White Star Publishers® is a registered trademark
property of De Agostini Libri S.p.A.

© 2015 De Agostini Libri S.p.A.
Via G. da Verrazano, 15
28100 Novara, Italy
www.whitestar.it - www.deagostini.it

Translation: ICEIGEO (Jonathan West), Milan

All rights reserved. No part of this publication may be reproduced,
stored in a retrieval system or transmitted in any form or by any means,
electronic, mechanical, photocopying, recording or otherwise,
without written permission from the publisher.

ISBN 978-88-544-1005-3
1 2 3 4 5 6   19 18 17 16 15

Printed in China